Steele, Philip,
1948-

Food & feasts in
ancient Rome.

$14.95

FOOD & FEASTS

IN

ANCIENT ROME

Philip Steele

New York

First American publication 1994 by New Discovery Books, Macmillan Publishing Company, 866 Third Avenue, New York, NY 10022

Macmillan Publishing Company is part of the Maxwell Communication Group of Companies.

First published in 1994 in Great Britain by Wayland (Publishers) Ltd

A ZOË BOOK

Devised and produced by
Zoë Books Limited
15 Worthy Lane
Winchester
Hampshire SO23 7AB
England

Printed in Belgium by Proost N.V.

Design: Jan Sterling, Sterling Associates
Picture research: Victoria Sturgess
Map: Gecko Limited
Production: Grahame Griffiths

10 9 8 7 6 5 4 3 2 1

Library of Congress Cataloging-in-Publication Data

Steele, Philip. 1948-
    Food & feasts in ancient Rome / Philip Steele.
        p. cm. — (Food & feasts)
    Includes index.
    ISBN 0-02-726321-5
    1. Diet—Rome—Juvenile literature. 2. Cookery, Roman—Juvenile literature. 3. Food habits—Rome—Juvenile literature. [1. Food habits—Rome. 2. Rome—Social life and customs. 3. Cookery, Roman.] I. Title. II. Series.
TX360.R64S73 1994
394.1'2'0937—dc20   93-28384

Summary: A social history of life in Ancient Rome, explaining why certain foods were eaten and how they were eaten. Includes information about the events that brought about special celebrations, and how these celebrations can be re-created today.

Photographic acknowledgments

The publishers wish to acknowledge, with thanks, the following photographic sources:

Ancient Art & Architecture Collection 6b, 10t & b, 14t, 21, 22t, 24b; The Bridgeman Art Library / Lauros-Giraudon 9; Corinium Museum, Cirencester 12; La Cour d'Or, Musées de Metz 6t; C.M.Dixon title page, 3, 4, 5b, 7, 8br, 13t & b, 14b, 16, 17t & b, 18t & b, 19t & b, 20t & br, 22b, 24t, 25t & b; English Heritage / Hadrian's Wall Museums 23t; Roger Goodburn 8bl; Mansell Collection 5t, 8t, 23b; Musée des Antiquités Nationales,© photo R.M.N. 15t; Museum of London 15b; Somerset County Museum 11; Werner Forman Archive / Pompeii Museum 20bl.

Cover: Ancient Art & Architecture Collection bottom left; C.M.Dixon top, center & bottom right

The publishers have made every effort to trace the copyright holders, but if they have inadvertently overlooked any, they will be pleased to make the necessary arrangement at the first opportunity.

CONTENTS

INTRODUCTION

N

0 100 300 500 miles
0 200 400 600 800 km

Key
The extent of the Roman Empire

North Sea

BRITAIN

Atlantic Ocean   Londinium

GERMANY

• Augusta Treverorum

GAUL

IBERIA   Massilia

•Emerita Augusta

Black Sea

ITALY   **DALMATIA**

ROME■   Herculaneum

Pompeii•

ANATOLIA

GREECE
Athens•

Aegean Sea

Carthago•

Mediterranean Sea

NORTH AFRICA

EGYPT   Alexandria

•Jerusalem

The Roman Empire around AD 250

▽ A young boy slave brings food to a noble family. Not all Romans ate the same food. Their diet depended on whether they were rich or poor, whether they lived in the town or the country, and whether they were free people or slaves.

More than 2,800 years ago a group of thatched huts was built on a hillside in western Italy. The people lived by hunting and farming. As the years went by, this settlement grew and grew. By A.D. 250 the city of Rome was home to more than a million people.

The Romans conquered lands in Europe and in Africa. Rome lay at the center of an **empire** that stretched from Spain to Syria, from North Africa to Britain. Merchant ships brought food from all over the empire to the port of Ostia, at the mouth of the Tiber River.

In order to feed so many hungry mouths, food production had to be highly organized. It became one of the Romans most

△ The Romans conquered many regions of Europe. They brought with them their own plants and ways of farming. In turn, they enjoyed the food of the lands where they settled.

Food for Rome

Pork was a specialty of Gaul (France).

Pickles were made in Iberia (Spain).

Fine wines were shipped through Massilia (Marseille).

Fruits were brought from the Greek islands.

Spices came from distant lands beyond the empire, such as India, China, and Southeast Asia. They included pepper, ginger, nutmeg, cinnamon, and cloves.

△ In A.D. 79 the volcano Vesuvius erupted. Ash and mud buried two Roman towns, Pompeii and Herculaneum. Among the ruins many everyday items of food were found. Eggs, figs, olives, walnuts, sausage, cakes, and bread have all been discovered there. Bread made in the region today looks much the same as it did more than 1,900 years ago.

important industries. Many thousands of people worked in farming, fishing, and **market gardening**. Others made their living as cooks, butchers, bakers, and shopkeepers.

History books often tell us about famous Roman soldiers, such as Julius Caesar. They do not often tell us about the people who farmed the land. And yet it was they who fed both the army and the other people, the **civilians**. Their work made the Roman Empire possible. The need for more rich farmland and new supplies of food was one reason why the Romans invaded other lands. The Romans established their way of life in most places under their control. Even when the Roman Empire finally collapsed in A.D. 476, the Roman way of life was not forgotten.

▽ At the time of the emperor Augustus (63 B.C.-A.D. 14) the city of Rome used 14 million **bushels** of grain every year. Wheat was shipped into Ostia from Carthage and Alexandria.

Farming and Country Fare

Country feasts

A Roman poet named Ovid (43 B.C.-A.D. 17) retold a Greek legend about an old country couple called Philemon and Baucis. They entertained the god Jupiter in their cottage, without realizing who he was. Ovid described the meal that the couple served to the god. It gives us some idea of how country people might have feasted in those days.

▽ In Roman times, as today, olives were an important crop in the Mediterranean region. Large presses extracted the oil, which was used in sauces as well as for cooking. Here, a farmer prunes his olive trees.

The first course was of baked eggs and cheese. Chickens and geese were kept on both large Roman estates and **smallholdings**. The cheese would have been made from goats' or sheep's milk rather than cows' milk.

△ To fashionable city dwellers, country table manners seemed rough and ready. In Roman cities, rich people ate lying down, on long couches. Country people often ate sitting down, in the manner of slaves or foreigners. This picture shows a family meal in Roman Gaul.

The main dish was boiled bacon. The couple might have kept their own pig, which would have ranged freely in the oak woods, eating acorns. Cabbage, mint, and a salad of **endives** and radishes were served, as well as juicy olives.

For dessert there were grapes, figs, plums, and apples, and a honeycomb from the beehive. The Romans did not know about sugar and used honey as a sweetener.

A meal like this would have been served only on a special occasion. Poor farm workers would often have little more than a bowl of thin barley **gruel** or a hunk of coarse bread and cheese. By way of thanks, Jupiter turned Philemon and Baucis into two trees, with intertwined branches, when they died!

The winter feast

In the early days of Rome, country people held a series of festivals between December 17 and 23. These were called "Saturnalia," in honor of the god Saturn.

Soon all Romans were joining in these celebrations. The high point was a huge meal that lasted all day. Slaves, too, could eat their fill and were waited upon by their masters.

▽ This picture was found in a Roman church. It is more than 1,600 years old. It shows the grapes being brought in from the vineyards in autumn.

△ Some farms were rented to tenants. Tenant farmers often paid their rent in kind, giving the landlord a share of their harvest or a supply of meat.

Working the land

Today, in many areas the landscape of western Europe is made up of wide, open fields, plowed by tractors. In Roman times, fields were smaller and plows were pulled by oxen. Much of the land was still covered in thick forest.

Most farms were little more than smallholdings, covering only about 1.25 acres of land. Soldiers were often rewarded for their service with a patch of land. During the conquest of northern Europe, soldiers would set up

▽ Flocks of sheep grazed the hills around many villas. They provided lamb and mutton as well as milk, **curds**, and cheeses.

▽ The Romans built a large **villa** at Chedworth, in England's Cotswold Hills. It was at the center of a big agricultural estate. Most villas had their own farm buildings, orchards, and vegetable gardens.

▷ Apples are picked from a villa's orchards in Gaul. The Romans were experts at growing fruit. They brought many new trees to northern Europe from Italy. Plums, pears, and walnuts were probably introduced into Britain in Roman times.

An easy life?

"How blessed beyond all blessings are farmers..." wrote the poet Virgil (70-19 B.C.). "Far from the clash of arms, the most just earth brings them an easy living from the soil." Country people might not have agreed! They had to work harder and longer hours than most city dwellers.

smallholdings in the countryside around a Roman fort when they retired from active service. They were protected by the army during times of trouble, and they could sell their produce to the soldiers.

In Italy and elsewhere in the empire, most food was produced on large estates. The land-owner was often absent, living in Rome or some other big city. The estate would be run by a manager, or **bailiff**. At the center of many country estates was a large house, or villa. Its wealthy owners brought their city ways to the countryside, dining in style with invited guests.

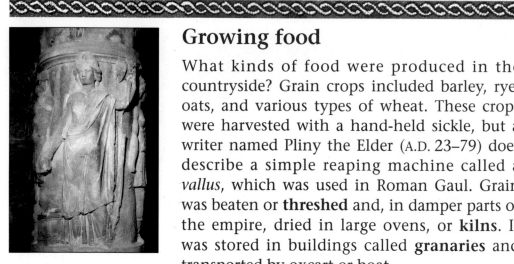

△ Many Roman gods and goddesses were connected with farming and the countryside. Ceres was the corn goddess. Our word "cereals" is derived from her name.

Growing food

What kinds of food were produced in the countryside? Grain crops included barley, rye, oats, and various types of wheat. These crops were harvested with a hand-held sickle, but a writer named Pliny the Elder (A.D. 23–79) does describe a simple reaping machine called a *vallus*, which was used in Roman Gaul. Grain was beaten or **threshed** and, in damper parts of the empire, dried in large ovens, or **kilns**. It was stored in buildings called **granaries** and transported by oxcart or boat.

Beans, peas, lentils, and other **pulses** were widely grown, as well as root vegetables such as turnips and carrots, and green vegetables including broccoli, celery, and leeks. Many vegetables were tougher and stringier than today's varieties. Some needed to be mashed or pulped before they could be served. The Romans did not, of course, grow the crops of the Americas, which were then unknown. They had never seen potatoes, tomatoes, or corn.

Regional favorites

Cheese from central Italy.
Wine from southern Italy. The most popular was Falernian.
Olives from the Sabine region, northeast of Rome.
Game from the forests around Rome.

▽ The *vallus* was used for reaping. It was pushed by a donkey into the stalks. The ears of wheat were cut off and fell into the scoop.

▷ Romans loved to hunt for deer or wild boar. Special game parks were sometimes set aside for use by hunters. People chased, or coursed, hares with dogs and hunted wildfowl on the marshes. Small birds were caught with nets, limed twigs, or bows and arrows.

Cows, sheep, pigs, and goats were raised on Roman farms. Pork was probably the most popular meat. Pigeons, pheasants, partridges, geese, and chickens were also reared. Farm produce included sausages made from the animals' internal organs, or **offal**, and creamy milk curds flavored with herbs.

Fishing was carried out along every coast and river of the empire. The Mediterranean Sea provided anchovies and tuna. Mussels and oysters were transported inland in barrels of salted water, called **brine**.

Wild nettles

Country people gathered wild plants for cooking and for medicines. Pliny described how nettle roots were boiled with meat to make it tender. Nettle tea was drunk to soothe aches and rheumatic pains.

▷ A Roman kitchen has been rebuilt at Cirencester in England. It is easy to imagine slaves preparing a feast for an invited guest. Slaves would carry buckets of water from the well and fuel for the stove. The cook would be chopping vegetables and herbs or skinning hares.

Country kitchens

Produce would be carried to a country kitchen in baskets or unloaded from a donkey. Supplies were stored in large pottery jars, which the cook often labeled with the contents. Tall jars with handles, called **amphorae**, contained wine or olive oil. They could be stored in racks or stuck into the ground.

Hares and wildfowl were hung on the kitchen wall. As today, pheasants were kept until they developed a strong flavor, or were "high." There were no canned, packaged, or frozen foods in Roman times. Foods were prevented from going bad, or **preserved**, by drying, pickling, smoking, or salting.

In the countryside, water had to be carried from the nearest fresh spring or well. Country people ground their own flour. They used small disks of rough stone, called **querns**, which were turned by hand. They also baked their own bread.

Poor people cooked for themselves, but rich country landowners kept slaves in their villa

△ Kitchens were cluttered with pots and pans made of clay, bronze, and iron. There were ladles, strainers, griddles, stewing pots, cleavers, pastry cutters, pestles, and mortars. Some of these utensils would not look out of place in many modern kitchens.

kitchens. Good cooks were expensive and were highly valued.

Kitchens might include a stone-built bread oven. Meat was sometimes roasted on a **spit**, in a sunken pit. Raised hearths built of brick were used for boiling and stewing. Care must have been taken to keep the fire glowing brightly. There were no chimneys to carry away smoke from the kitchen.

◁ This bronze strainer looks very much like a modern one. It was found at Trier, in Germany. In Roman times this town was called Augusta Treverorum.

DINING IN TOWNS AND CITIES

Food for the city

A young country girl visiting her relatives in Rome would have found life there very different from life at home. Although farm carts were banned from the streets during the day, the city was still crowded and noisy. Market traders and shopkeepers shouted to people to tell them what was for sale.

City dwellers relied on these shops — the **retail trade** — for their food supply. The streets around the town center, or **forum**, were lined with markets and shops. Today, we can tell the streets that contained certain shops. Fragments of wine flagons, piles of mussel or oyster shells, and bones from butchers' shops have been dug up by people who study the past — the **archaeologists**.

As well as produce that was brought into Italy, or **imported**, through Ostia, Rome received supplies from the surrounding countryside. There were also market gardens and vineyards within the city. Wealthy people grew fruit trees and herbs in their town

△ This woman has set up her fruit stall by the side of the road.

▽ A butcher prepares a choice cut of meat. Beef was the most expensive meat and so was less popular with customers.

▷ A baker places bread in his oven. Loaves came in all shapes and flavors — round or square, thick or thin, seeded or spiced.

▽ These Roman scales were found in London, England. A public office of weights and measures was at the center of the town of Pompeii.

gardens. Popular herbs included mint, **lovage**, and **rue**.

In the city there were large **commercial** bakeries. Bakers used horses to turn the huge millstones that ground the grain into flour. Flour was whitened artificially, and often cheap substances were added to bulk it out. These tricks have been used by the food industry even in the 20th century.

Free bread

In 123 B.C. a politician named Gaius Gracchus ordered cut-price grain for poor people in Rome. By 71 B.C. it was given out free, and later lard and oil were added to this "gift." It cost the state a fortune, but riots broke out whenever it was stopped.

Eating habits

Most Romans ate three times during the day. However, many poor people and slaves often went hungry. They ate gruel instead of bread, and drank water or cheap sour wine.

Breakfast (*ientaculum*) was eaten early (except by the lazy!). It was a simple meal, perhaps bread and cheese, or leftovers from the night before.

Lunch (*prandium*) was eaten around noon or later. This was a light, informal meal, when cold rather than hot food was often served. When Vesuvius erupted in A.D. 79, many people in Pompeii and Herculaneum were just sitting down to lunch — chicken, eggs, and lentils were on the menu.

Some city dwellers probably ate lunch at inns or **taverns**, ordering sausages, fried fish, or salads. Even then the Romans were making dishes rather like the Italian favorites, pizza and pasta, of today.

Dinner (still called *cena* in Italy) was the most important meal of the day. It was served in the dining room (*triclinium*) early or late in the evening, after the master of the house had finished his afternoon session at the public baths.

For many Romans dinner was a modest meal. However, for the

▽ Many people probably bought snacks on their way to work. Stalls and shops sold bread, hot pies, pastries, and sweets, as well as cheeses, olives, nuts, and figs.

richest people it was often an excuse for incredible greed and **gluttony**. Some Roman emperors stayed at their tables from noon until midnight, eating until they were sick and then starting all over again.

◁ Cooks spent most of the day preparing *cena*, the hot evening meal. These Roman cooks are shown in a picture uncovered at Trier, in Germany.

▽ A wall painting from Pompeii shows a maid bringing food.

Dinner for two

This modest *cena* was offered by a poet named Martial, who came to Rome from Spain in A.D. 64. The guest was his friend Toranius.

APPETIZERS

Wine sweetened with honey
Leeks and lettuce
Tuna with egg

MAIN COURSE

Broccoli
Sausage
Bacon with beans
Wine

DESSERT

Raisins, pears,
chestnuts

△ The name *triclinium* means a "three-couch room." This fine example was uncovered at Herculaneum.

At the table

In cities, the *triclinium* was often smaller than in some spacious country villas, many of which had separate dining rooms for summer and winter.

Some dining rooms were splendidly decorated. There might be wall paintings and floor pictures made up of tiny pieces of colored tiles, called **mosaics**. These often served as conversation pieces during the dinner. One wall at Pompeii includes notes on table manners. Guests are warned not to argue and to avoid bad language and flirtation. However, belching and spitting at the table were generally accepted!

▽ This lovely silver bowl was found at Mildenhall in England, along with many other items of Roman tableware.

△ Some tableware was made of pottery. These cups from Roman Gaul were found at Nîmes. Pottery drinking cups were sometimes decorated with mottoes such as "Drink me dry!" or "Long life!"

▽ The Romans made glass jugs and bowls.

Dinner guests were announced at the door. They removed their sandals, then a slave washed their feet. Dress was a lightweight gown called a *synthesis*, although best clothes were worn if dining with important people or the emperor. A low table was surrounded on three sides by draped couches with cushions. Extra tables were provided for large **banquets**.

The host and hostess lay on the couch of honor, in the center. Honored guests lay on the host's right. The children sat on low stools at the side.

Tablecloths became fashionable during the reign of Domitian, who became emperor in A.D. 81. Guests brought their own napkins. These could be filled with food and taken home after the meal.

▷ Roman cutlery included knives, spoons, and toothpicks. There were no forks. Most food was cut up before being brought in from the kitchen. Guests ate with their fingers, which were washed by slaves with jugs of water.

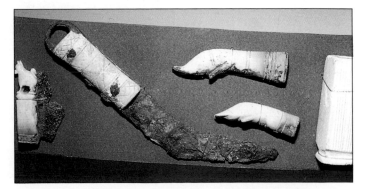

Food for a banquet

▷ At this banquet in Pompeii, a drunken guest is helped from the room. A statesman named Cato the Elder recommended pickled cabbage as a cure for an upset stomach or hangover!

Most dinners were of three courses, but a full banquet might include seven or eight courses. There were three main types of dishes. The *gustatio* (appetizers) would include eggs and salad or shellfish. The *fercula*, prepared dishes brought in from the kitchen, might include stuffed pork, veal, beef, or **venison** served with vegetables. The dessert, or *mensae secundae*, often included fruit, dates, and honey cakes.

Special delicacies included fattened dormice, small birds such as thrushes and figpeckers, milk-fed snails, **truffles**, and ice-cream made from snow mixed with flour and sweet white wine. Some rich people valued dishes because they were unusual, not because they were tasty. They served peacock brains,

▽ Slaves brought in dishes from the kitchen and waited on guests. At Trimalchio's feast there were singing waiters!

▽ Food and drink were kept warm for the table in elaborate urns, rather like the *samovars* used in Russia today.

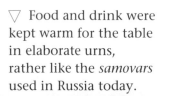

ostrich flesh, flamingo tongues, and bear cutlets.

The Romans loved sweet and sour flavors. Their food was spiced and peppery and was full of herbs. There were many sauces. Oysters were served with an egg sauce, or **mayonnaise**, made of egg yolk, pepper, vinegar, oil, wine, and lovage. The most popular sauce, served with all kinds of meat, was a salty mixture of fish guts. These were allowed to go slightly moldy, until they **fermented**. *Garum* was a coarse fish sauce, while *liquamen* was strained smooth. Sauces like these are popular today in Southeast Asia.

▽ Wine was normally served mixed with water. It was often spiced with pepper or sweetened with honey. It might be served warmed or chilled. Cellars were packed with ice to make a cold storage place.

Entertainment

Between courses, diners might be entertained by jugglers, acrobats, clowns, dancers, and musicians. Guests were sometimes showered with rose petals. Many poorer Romans disapproved of such luxury.

Trimalchio's feast

A writer named Petronius (d. A.D. 66) made fun of an extravagant banquet given by a rich man he called Trimalchio. The many dishes included:

Honeyed dormice with poppy seed

Hare with sow's udders

Boiled calf

Figpeckers in pastry made to look like peahen's eggs

Stuffed thrushes and quinces made to look like sea urchins

A boar served with "piglets" of marzipan

A "goose," "birds," and "fish" that were really made of pork

FOOD FOR TRAVELERS

△ Soldiers on the march carried **rations**, mess tins, and buckets on a pole over their shoulders.

On the road

The Romans built fine paved roads across their empire. People traveled in oxcarts, in light horse-drawn wagons, or on mules. They might stay and dine with friends on the way. In remote areas they might sleep outdoors, perhaps lighting a campfire and catching a hare for the pot. There were wayside taverns across the empire, and sometimes villages and towns grew up around these stopping places.

In large Roman towns there were special sleeping rooms for travelers, called *hospitalia*. When important people traveled across the empire they stayed at official rest houses, or *mansiones*.

On the road, people might eat biscuits, dates, figs, or olives. Food could be bought from shops and roadside stalls.

Merchants, sailors, and soldiers traveled throughout the known world. The Roman **legions** tramped the length and breadth of the empire. Italian troops marched alongside Africans, Spaniards, Celts from Gaul and Britain, and Germans. Many of them continued to eat

▽ Food for travelers had to be easy to carry. It was packed into baskets on carts or carried in saddlebags on mules.

◁ Roman troops in Britain consumed about 20,000 tons of wheat a year. This grain measure was found on the northern frontier, at Hadrian's Wall. Records and written accounts list items supplied to troops on the wall. They include wheat, barley, spices, salt, fish sauce, pork, roedeer, lard, vintage wine, sour wine, and beer.

and drink in their own way, preferring beer to sour wine, for example.

On campaign, soldiers were issued their food allowance, or rations, for 3 to 15 days. These included hard biscuits, sour wine, salt, and preserved foods such as bacon and cheese.

▷ When fighting, the Roman army would seize cattle, poultry, grain, or horsefodder from enemy villages and camps.

European cooking

Travelers and settlers spread the Roman way of cooking across the empire. Many of the dishes eaten in Europe today were known 2,000 years ago, in Roman times.

Many modern words for food come from Latin, the language spoken by the ancient Romans. These words passed into other languages. For example, Welsh is a Celtic language that developed from the language spoken by the Britons during the Roman Empire. Another Celtic language was spoken in Gaul. See how many of the words below look similar.

Latin	English	Italian	Spanish	German	French	Dutch	Welsh
coquere	to cook	*cuocere*	*cocinar*	*kochen*	*cuire*	*koken*	*coginio*
fructus	fruit	*frutto*	*fruta*	*Frucht*	*fruit*	*vrucht*	*ffrwyth*
vinum	wine	*vino*	*vino*	*Wein*	*vin*	*wijn*	*gwin*
piper	pepper	*pepe*	*pimiento*	*Pfeffer*	*poivre*	*peper*	*pupur*
oleum	oil	*olio*	*aceite*	*Ol*	*huile*	*olie*	*olew*
caepe	—	*cipolla*	*cebolla*	*Zwiebel*	*ciboule*	—	*sibol*
unio	onion	—	—	—	*oignon*	*ui*	*nionyn*

Taverns and bars

While many travelers dined at inns and rest houses, others ate and drank at smaller restaurants, taverns, and bars. Some of these were used by respectable travelers, but others were popular with rowdy sailors and small-time criminals. In busy ports, drunken customers would quarrel, gamble with dice, and scribble rude messages or sayings, **graffiti**, on the walls.

△ This picture from Mérida, Spain, shows a barmaid in a tavern drawing wine from a cask.

▽ The bars in Pompeii contained holes for covered pottery jars.

▷ This picture shows Bacchus, the Roman god of wine. It was found in a Roman villa in Corinth, Greece. The ancient Greek name for the god was Dionysos.

The taverns sold wine, which was often mixed with hot water. Hot snacks, such as sweet-and-sour meats, were served from jars set into the bar, which was made of marble. At the back of the tavern were stone tables and benches. Guests would eat sitting or lying down, while servants brought jugs of wine.

◁ A Roman mosaic from North Africa shows gamblers throwing dice in a tavern.

COOK THE ROMAN WAY

The best known Roman cookbook was called *De Re Coquinaria* (*On Cooking*). It was written by a man who appreciated good food, a **gourmet**, named Apicius. Several people of this name lived in ancient Rome. One of them taught cooking about 2,000 years ago. His recipes were written down and added to 400 years later.

It is said that having spent a vast fortune on good eating, Apicius was down to his last 10 million *sesterces* (about $225,000). Complaining that this sum was only enough to fill his stomach with dull, ordinary fare, he decided to poison himself!

Roman recipes can be tried out today. Many of the ingredients can still be bought, especially in Indian or Chinese grocery stores. However, some herbs or spices are hard to find, so more common ones may be used instead. Anchovy essence, soy sauce, or oriental fish sauce may be used instead of *liquamen*.

> **WARNING:** Sharp knives and boiling liquids are dangerous. Hot ovens and pans can burn you. *Always ask an adult to help you* when you are preparing or cooking food in the kitchen.

CELERY AND LEEKS IN HONEY SAUCE

Ingredients
6 sticks celery
$^1/_2$ cup water
8 leeks
1 tsp ground pepper
$^1/_2$ cup bouillon
2 tsp clear honey

Equipment
cutting board
sharp knife
2 saucepans
measuring cup
colander
serving bowl

1. Cut the celery into small pieces, taking care to keep your fingers away from the blade of the knife. Place in a saucepan and add the water. Bring to a boil and simmer for 15 minutes. Remove the celery but keep the cooking liquid.
2. Clean the leeks, carefully cut into pieces and place in another saucepan. Cover with more water, cook until tender and then drain.
3. To make the sauce, add pepper, bouillon, and honey to the cooking liquid from the

celery. Bring this back to a boil over a low heat and allow it to simmer for 25 minutes.

4. Put the cooked leeks into a clean pan, add the celery sections, and pour the sauce over them.
5. Heat them through and then serve in a warmed serving dish.

AUTUMN FEAST

1. Butter a baking dish. Carefully peel and dice the pumpkin, discarding the seeds. Peel, core, and chop the apples. Mix the vegetables and place in the prepared dish.
2. Make a sauce by mixing together the mint leaves, honey, bouillon, vinegar, and pepper. Pour over the pumpkin and apple mixture.
3. Bake for 30 minutes in a pre-heated 350°F oven. Ask an adult to place the baking dish in the oven and to take it out when it is cooked. Sprinke with ginger just before serving.

Ingredients
1 tsp butter
small pumpkin
2 cooking apples
sprig mint
1 T honey
$\frac{1}{4}$ cup bouillon
1 T white wine vinegar
pepper
1 tsp ground ginger

Equipment
baking dish
sharp knife
cutting board
measuring cup
bowl

ROMAN CHICKEN

1. Remove any giblets and place the chicken in a large saucepan. Cover chicken with water. Bring to a boil and simmer gently for $2\frac{1}{2}$-3 hours. Make sure that the saucepan does not boil dry.
2. To make the sauce, you will need a mortar and pestle. Mix and grind all the herbs and spices in this.
3. Add the vinegar and the dates to the spice mixture, pounding to a smooth paste.
4. Transfer the paste to a mixing bowl and stir in the honey, oil, and anchovy essence *or* soy sauce. Add sufficient liquid from the chicken to give a thick pouring consistency.
5. Ask an adult to remove the chicken from the pan and place on a serving plate. Pour the sauce over the chicken and eat at once *or* leave the chicken to cool and eat the dish cold.

Ingredients
1 boiling chicken
a pinch each of:
    pepper, cumin, thyme, rue *or* rosemary, mint, fennel
tiny drop of asafoetida (available from Indian grocery stores)
2 T vinegar
4 oz ($\frac{2}{3}$ cup) stoned and chopped dates
1 T honey
1 T olive oil
1 tsp anchovy essence (*or* soy sauce)

Equipment
large saucepan
mortar and pestle
measuring cup
mixing bowl
serving dish

DATES WITH ALMONDS

Ingredients
24 dates
2 tsp salt
24 blanched
    almonds
1 tsp cinnamon
1 T olive oil
³/₄ cup clear honey

1. Carefully slit the dates down one side and remove the pits. Rub the dates with salt.
2. Sprinkle the almonds with cinnamon. Put an almond inside each date.
3. Heat the oil in a skillet and pour in the honey. Warm over a low heat.
4. Add the dates and heat them through quickly. Put them in a dish and serve at once.

Equipment
sharp knife
cutting board
measuring cup
skillet
serving dish

Sharp knives and hot oil are dangerous.

ROMAN TOAST

Ingredients
3 T olive oil
4 thick slices white
    bread
¹/₂ cup milk
2 T clear honey

Ask an adult to help you when you start to cook.

1. Pour the oil into a skillet and place over a very low heat. Take care that the oil does not start to burn.
2. Slice the bread and cut off the crusts. Put the milk into a shallow dish and quickly dip the slices of bread in and out of the milk.
3. Transfer the bread to the skillet and fry until lightly browned on both sides.
4. Spread the fried bread with honey and serve.

Equipment
skillet
bread knife
bread board
measuring cup
shallow dish
serving plates

NUTTY OMELET

Ingredients
¹/₄ cup blanched
    almonds
1 tsp honey
ground pepper
¹/₂ tsp anchovy
    essence (*or* soy
    sauce)
¹/₃ cup milk
5 large eggs
2 tsp butter

1. Place the nuts on a baking sheet and put in a pre-heated 325°F oven. Leave for 20 minutes. Ask an adult to take it in and out of the oven for you.
2. While the nuts are cooling down, whisk the eggs well in a mixing bowl.
3. Mix the honey, pepper, and milk with the well-beaten eggs.
4. Chop the nuts very carefully with a sharp knife or ask an adult to coarsely chop them in a food processor. Add them to the egg mixture. Stir in the anchovy essence *or* soy sauce.
5. Melt the butter in a skillet and pour in the mixture.
6. Cook carefully on low heat and turn the omelet over with a spatula. Cook until well done on both sides.

Equipment
baking sheet
measuring cup
mixing bowl
whisk
sharp knife
cutting board
skillet
spatula
plates or serving dish

Ask an adult to help you when you start to cook.

ROMAN CUSTARD

Ingredients
2 cups milk
¼ cup clear honey
3 egg yolks
¼ tsp nutmeg

1. Pour the milk into a bowl and mix with the honey.
2. Whisk the egg yolks in a separate bowl.
3. Pour the milk mixture into a saucepan and heat briefly.
4. Take it off the heat and add the well-beaten egg yolks. Add the nutmeg and stir thoroughly.
5. Pour into a baking dish and bake in a pre-heated oven at 325°F. It should set within an hour. Ask an adult to take it in and out of the oven for you.

Equipment
measuring cup
2 mixing bowls
whisk
saucepan
wooden spoon
baking dish

Hot liquids, pans and ovens are dangerous.

SWEET WINE CAKES

Ingredients
1²/₃ cups self-rising flour
¼ cup shortening
¼ cup grated cheese
1 egg
1 T sweet white wine (*or* grape juice)
pinch each of whole aniseed and cumin seeds
12 bay leaves

1. Sift the flour into a mixing bowl.
2. Cut the shortening into small pieces and, using your fingers, rub into the flour with the cheese. The mixture should look like fresh breadcrumbs.
3. Whisk the egg in another bowl and add to the flour mixture with the sweet white wine *or* grape juice and the spices. Blend in with a wooden spoon.
4. Shape the mixture into 12 small cakes and place each on a bay leaf.
5. Place on a baking sheet and put in a pre-heated oven at 400°F for about 25-30 minutes. Ask an adult to take it in and out of the oven for you.

Equipment
measuring cup
sieve
1 large mixing bowl
knife
1 small mixing bowl
whisk
baking sheet
cooling rack
wooden spoon
plate

GLOSSARY

amphora:
(pl. **amphorae**)
 A tall, narrow jar made of pottery, used to store liquids such as wine.

archaeologist:
 Someone who studies the past by digging up or examining ancient ruins and remains.

bailiff:
 The overseer or manager of a country estate.

banquet:
 A grand feast or public dinner.

brine:
 Salted water, used for pickling.

bushel:
 A measure of capacity — one bushel is about 32 quarts.

civilian:
 Somebody who is not a soldier.

commercial:
 To do with business — buying and selling.

curds:
 A sour, creamy dish like yogurt. It is part of the cheese-making process.

empire:
 A group of countries ruled by a single government or by an emperor.

endive:
 A green plant used in salads.

fermented:
 Chemically changed by a natural organism such as yeast (which turns sugar into alcohol).

forum:
 The central square and chief meeting place in a Roman town, occupied by official buildings, temples, and markets.

gluttony:
 Overeating. The greediest Roman emperor was Vitellius, who ruled briefly in A.D. 69. At one dinner in his honor, 2,000 fish and 7,000 birds were served!

gourmet:
 Somebody who appreciates the best food and drink.

graffiti:
 Words or pictures scribbled or painted on walls or public statues.

granary:
 A building used to store grain.

gruel:
 A thin soup or porridge made of boiled grains.

import:
 To bring goods into a country, in return for other goods or payment.

kiln:
 A large furnace used for baking, burning, or drying.

legion:
 A group of soldiers, numbering between 3,000 and 6,000.

lovage:
 A strong, spicy herb, popular in Roman cooking and medicine.

market gardening:
 Growing vegetables, fruit, and herbs for sale. Market gardens were large and often fenced off or walled.

mayonnaise:	A salad dressing made of eggs, olive oil, and vinegar.
mosaic:	A picture made from tiny chips of colored stone or glass.
offal:	The parts of an animal removed during butchering, such as kidneys, heart, lungs, stomach, or liver.
preserve:	To keep food from going bad by stopping the spread of bacteria. Foods can be preserved by drying, freezing, pickling, or keeping in airtight jars or cans.
pulse:	The seed of a plant such as peas, beans, or lentils, eaten as food.
quern:	A stone handmill, once used for grinding grain into flour.
rations:	Limited amounts of food, such as those issued to soldiers or sailors.
retail trade:	The selling of goods directly to the public, through shops or markets. The selling of produce to the shopkeeper is called the wholesale trade.
rue:	A bitter herb widely used in Roman cooking.
smallholding:	A cottage with a patch of farmland, smaller than a normal farm.
spit:	A turning rod used to hold roasting meat over a fire or grill.
tavern:	An inn, serving drink and food.
thresh:	To separate grain from its stalk. Today this is done by machinery in most countries. In Roman times it was done by beating or by trampling.
truffle:	A delicious underground fungus. It is still regarded as a delicacy today.
venison:	Deer meat.
villa:	In Roman times, a large country house.

Further reading

Bisignano, Alphonse. *Cooking the Italian Way*. Minneapolis, Minnesota: Lerner Publishers, 1982.

Caselli, Giovanni. *The Roman Empire and the Dark Ages*. New York: Peter Bedrick Books, 1985.

Dineen, Jacqueline. *The Romans*. New York: New Discovery Books, 1992.

Gaspari, Claudia. *Food in Italy*. Vero Beach, Florida: Rourke Publishing Group, 1989.

Morley, Jacqueline and John James. *Roman Villa: Inside Story*. New York: Peter Bedrick Books, 1988.

INDEX